The Shepherds' Quest

by Daniel R. Colasanti, Sr.

Daniel R. Colasanti, Sr.

The Shepherds' Quest

Copyrights & Publishing

Dedication

This play is dedicated to my wife, Gemma Ann (Nacca) Colasanti, whose strong faith in God inspired me to write it.

I am very grateful for her encouragement and helpful critiques throughout the play's development, and for her boundless love throughout our journey together.

Nazareth – The Setting of God's Message to Mary

At the time of Jesus, Nazareth was a town in the province of Galilee in northern Israel, where a small community of Jews were living as farmers and tradesmen. Nazareth was set in a small basin surrounded by hills and wasn't very accessible. It did have a well, and there were some terraced agriculture and pasture fields.

Nazareth's wet season ran from mid-October to mid-April with the dry season from mid-June to mid-September, and although the dry season could get very hot during Summer, the cool breezes and low humidity at times made the Summers quite pleasant.

Being Jewish, men were commanded to know the Torah, the 5 books that contain the laws and teachings that God revealed to Moses and the Israelites. However, it was deemed unnecessary for women to read.

Mary was a peasant girl of about 14 years old that lived in a mud-brick house. While living at home, Mary and the women in the family worked together and shared everything. Besides the housework, the women also helped in the fields tending the crops, and participating in the yearly harvesting.

Although Joseph was older than Mary, he was well-regarded by the people of Nazareth as a righteous person and one suitable for marriage. At the time of their betrothal, Joseph was a carpenter by trade.

When Mary became of marriageable age, her whole family, selected Joseph, as her appropriate husband. The engagement contract made Mary very happy, since living in a small village, Joseph was someone she had known all her life, and perhaps was the man she always hoped to marry.

The Annunciation

An Angel Appears to Mary in Nazareth

ST. LUKE

Chapter 1
Verses 26-32, 38

NARRATOR:
" The angel Gabriel was sent from God to a town of Galilee called Nazareth,
To a virgin betrothed to a man named Joseph, of the House of David, and the virgin's name was
Mary. And when the angel had come to her, he said,"

ANGEL:
"Hail, full of grace, the Lord is with thee. Blessed art thou among women."

NARRATOR:
"When she had heard him she was troubled at his word, and kept pondering what manner of
greeting this might be. And the angel said to her,"

ANGEL:
"Do not be afraid, Mary, for thou hast found grace with God.
Behold, thou shalt conceive in thy womb and shalt bring forth a son;
And thou shalt call his name Jesus. He shall be great,
And shall be called the Son of the Most High;
And the Lord God will give him the throne of David his father,
And he shall be King over the House of Jacob forever;
And of his kingdom there shall be no end."

NARRATOR:
" Mary said, "

MARY:
"Behold the handmaid of the Lord; be it done to me according to thy word."

NARRATOR:
"And the angel departed from her

Acts and Other Information

Acts

Act 1

Scene 1: The Shepherds

Scene 2: The Work Day

Act 2

Scene 3: Shepherd's Faith Tested

Scene 4: Decisions & Journey

Act 3

Scene 5: The Visitation

Scene 6: The Message

Complementary Details

Nazareth

Bethlehem

**Poem by
Jan Mahannah**

Life after Jesus' birth

Supplemental Data

Play Credits

Foreword

In a small village, over two thousand years ago, a group of shepherds were alarmed by the presence of an angel that told them that the Messiah, who was foretold to come, was born in Bethlehem that night.

This play addresses the shepherds' lives and work. It imagines their innermost thoughts and feelings on that first Christmas Day - what they saw and considered that day, and as they later embarked upon their journey to visit the Christ Child.

The play also includes a story of a young couple in love whose prayers are answered shortly after the birth of Jesus.

Whereas the Biblical accounts in the play are factual, the events and relationships of the characters are a product of the author's imagination.

Besides being very educational, the play also describes the characters' lives after the birth of Jesus.

Bethlehem – The Setting of Jesus' Birth

"Kloster in Bethlehem,"
Painted in 1882 by Bernhard Fiedler.

A repurposed cave located under a first-century house excavated near Bethlehem. Carved into the upper part of the wall on the left is a row of small niches for holding oil lamps, and carved into the cave wall on the right is a row of feeding or watering troughs for animals.   Oren Gutfeld

Bethlehem was a typical Jewish village at the time of Jesus' birth with a population of about 3,000 people. It is situated on a hill almost 800 meters above the Mediterranean Sea. Its people lived in clans, usually in large one-room, or two-room, houses built around one of the many caves of Bethlehem's limestone hills.

The caves were often used for storage and to keep the family's animals of sheep, goats, and donkeys safe from the cold and thieves. Carvings made into the grotto walls provided small niches for oil lamps to provide dim interior light. Other carvings in the walls created large stone troughs to water the animals.

The slopes of Bethlehem's surrounding hills and their adjacent fields provided fertile agricultural lands for harvesting wheat and barley which likely gave the village its Hebrew name, "House of Bread."

The sloping hills also contained terraced orchards of olive trees, and the large stretches of natural brush in the countryside was ideal for local shepherds to graze flocks of sheep and goats.

Watchtowers made from stacked fieldstones provided security; and small immersion pools cut into the bedrock allowed agricultural workers to maintain the Biblical standards of ritual purity required to handle produce or animals that would be sent to the Temple.

Act 1, Scene 1 – The Shepherds

SHEPHERD:

We are all good shepherds that know our sheep and our sheep know us

Abel

Abel is in the fields east of Bethlehem tending Temple sheep
Abel is a young romantic, a great leader, and cares much for his family
He loves Anne dearly and is very concerned about his future

ABEL:
All of our tasks are like those other shepherds bear
While they tend their family's sheep
We tend the sheep of the Temple priests that are entrusted to our care
We too help our families from what we reap

There is no job that I would rather do
Than to be out each day in the fields of dew
With Jacob, my friend and mentor, who has seen me through
Also with sheep and shepherd friends that abide,
Faithful friends with me as their spokesperson and guide

Except for Jacob, I am just a few years older than they
Who must now manage well to do what is best for all
Hence, I pray to God for wisdom each day
For sound decisions, so they will not go astray

A Temple shepherd's job is one passed down
To the youngest child of the family
Older siblings work on their father's farm
To grow and harvest crops to store in his barn

But, when my days as a Temple shepherd ends
What will I do to make a living then?
There is no place for me on my father's farm

ABEL'S DOG ADA AND THE TEMPLE SHEEP

10

ABEL (CONT'D)

For my siblings already do what's needed in the fields and barn
God knows that I do not want to tend sheep of the wealthy lot
Who employ hired hands to tend their flocks
Shepherds like they cannot be trusted to care for the sheep each day
For hireling's only interest is their daily pay

Perhaps a builder's, stonecutter's, carpenter's, or potter's job could be mine
Jobs, we all know, to master them, takes much effort and time
But, really to remain a shepherd is what I want to be
In life with Anne, the sweet and faithful woman I often see

Anne, a beautiful girl, so mild, loving, and kind
Who is the wife, I pray, would one day be mine

High Priest

NARRATOR:

The High Priest was the supreme religious leader of the Israelites whose office was hereditary. He was considered to be the mediator and intercessor between God and his people.

Only he was allowed to wear the breastplate of engraved gemstones identifying the twelve tribes of Israel.

His most important duty was conducting the service on the day of Atonement, the tenth day of the seventh month of every year, which during that service he would cast away the sins of the people.

HIGH PRIEST:

Sheep that all shepherds daily tend
Are in pastures many miles from Bethlehem
For odors from large flocks do foul our town
But on Passover things are turned around

Thirty days before our most holy event
One year old, unblemished ewes are sent
To graze in the valley close to the Temple clan
On pastures owned by me, the High Priest
For the Temple's religious plan

In the middle of each of those pasture grounds
That run east and south of the cliffs of town
Is a 2-story "Watch Tower of Flock"
That priests climb daily to see all around
To watch over our shepherds and domesticated stock
From robbers, the wolf, the bear, and the lion

The towers keep the priests ritually clean
Whereas shepherds that step daily on soiled sod are not
Thus shepherds cannot participate in our religious events
Their religious life is just between them and God

Areas far removed from Bethlehem and the "Watch Towers of Flock"
Are places where Temple shepherds also tend
Today is one of them

A "WATCH TOWER OF FLOCK"

WATCH TOWER OF FLOCK (aka MIGDAL EDER)

BETHLEHEM

Pasture lands close to Bethlehem are owned by the High Priest

They are used only during the days of Passover

Pasture lands normally used by Temple and non-Temple shepherds daily are located several miles from Bethlehem

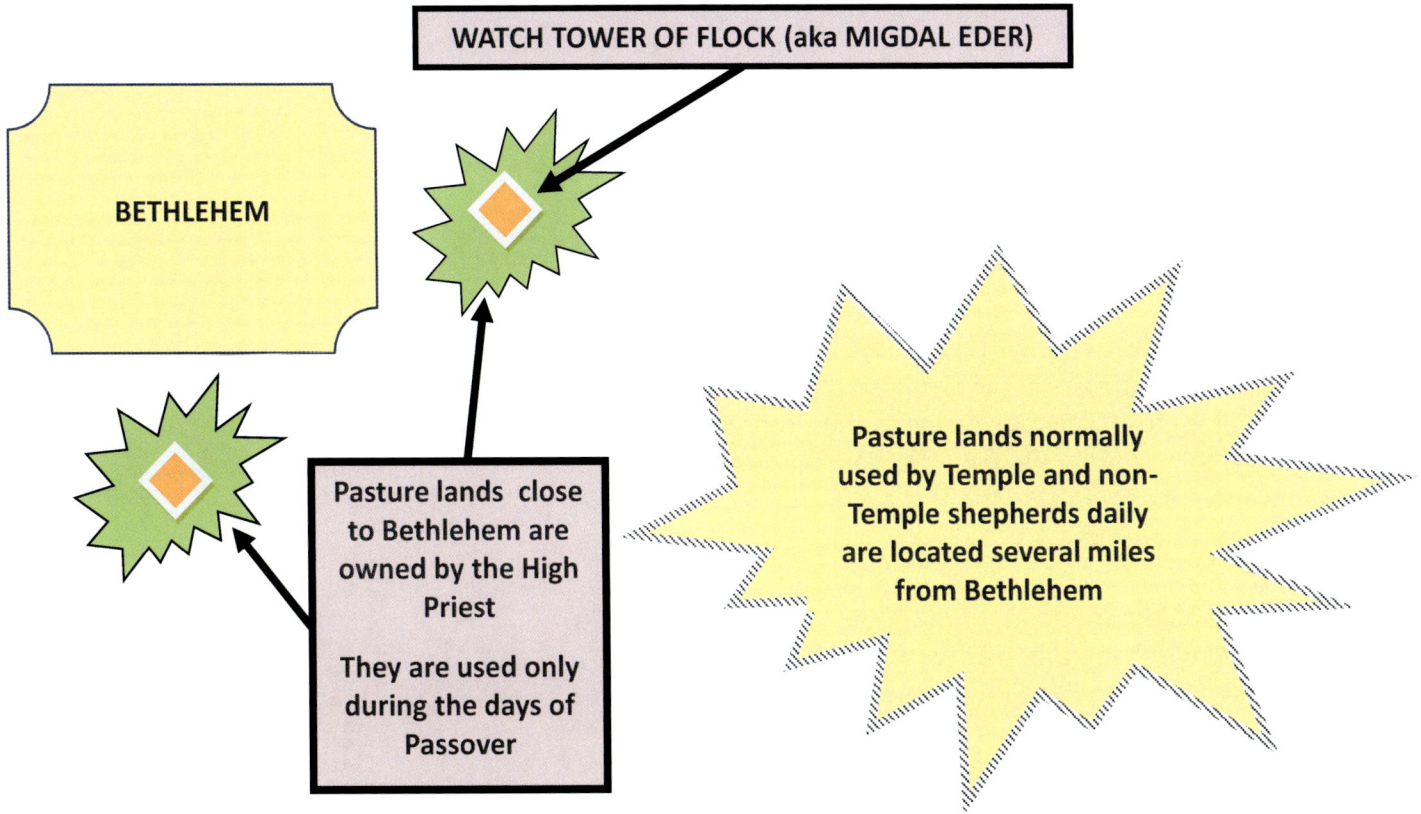

Temple SHEEP (EWES, RAMS, LAMBS, ALL WHITE, ALL AGES, ONE BREED)

Rachel

Rachel is Jacob's wife, dignified, and mature
She is motherly, understanding, strong and authoritative, but kind
Rachel is in a field near her husband Jacob where she sometimes tends her father's sheep
Jacob's and her father's fields are close to the Temple shepherd fields
Rachel can multi-task easily, caring for her husband's, children's, and parent's needs
She is loved by friends and family and willing to help out whenever the need arises
She loves to teach others

RACHEL:
Jacob is the oldest shepherd of our time
While he tends sheep that he owns
I tend sheep that are my father's sometimes
Joining with Jacob those days after a long climb
Everyone knows I am the only shepherdess of this time

The sheep that Temple shepherds tend are not their own
But rather those to be sacrificed by the Temple priests
The sheep to be declared holy and consecrated upon the throne
On days of Passover and those for peace

The Temple shepherds are trained for this noble task
Excluded from all religious acts
To tend the sheep all year long
Making sure that they themselves do no wrong

14

RACHEL (CONT'D):

All shepherds teach their dog and sheep to obey commands,
By assigning them names by sound
When calls are formed by mouth and hands
The dog will lead the sheep to the pasture ground

In spring, the fleece is sheared from the sheep
While in Summer the sheep are moved to higher cooler ground
Should a howl of a Hyena, or Jackal, panic the flock
The shepherd's reassuring voice calms them down

And, should the pools of rainwater dry up
The flock will be led to a well nearby,
Where water will be drawn for them to drink
After filling the troughs to the brink

In the evening the flocks will be led to the folds
And shepherds will count them as they pass under the rod the door holds
Then, the shepherds will guard the sheepfold throughout the night calm
From robbers and wild beasts that would do them harm

WELL USED WHEN
WATERING PLACES DRY UP

SHEEP CALLS

HYENA

JACKAL

PERMANENT AND TEMPORARY SHEEPFOLDS

Jacob

NARRATOR:
Jacob is the most senior shepherd in all of Bethlehem proper
He is not a Temple shepherd
He loves his wife Rachel and has been a mentor to Abel
Jacob owns hundreds of sheep and tends them in his field with his many sons
From experience, Jacob knows well what a shepherd's life is all about

Jacob's sheep and dog Noah

JACOB:

A shepherd's job is one I love
Outdoors each day with plenty of blue skies above
Carefree with no hired boss and good pay
With animals that like me, and I they

Our clothing is simple and robust
To protect us from rain and the cold night air
A mantle of sheepskin or camel hair
So too a cotton tunic, sandals, and woolen headwear

A staff and sling we also bring
Armaments that are necessary things
Together they provide the means for our sheep's protection
Keeping away the wild beasts and robbers that beckon

Our oak staff has a knob on top with sharp nails sticking from it
A few beatings are all it takes to make aggressors quit
The staff is also used to explore crevices around
To scare out any scorpions or snakes that abound

The sling, made of two sinew strings
Has a pouch for rocks that we can fling
At those that wish to do us harm
Like David and Goliath in the Bible psalm

We also carry a small bag made of dried skin
To hold the food that we'll eat that day
The bag can also carry several big stones
That we'll use with our sling to thrust them away

**SHEPHERD
AND HIS DOG**

**WELL,
BUCKET,
TROUGH,
AND BAG**

SLING

JACOB (CONT'D):

Toiling throughout the long and worrisome day
There is still time for prayer
And to play some music on our flutes of reed
For sheep and shepherds, it satisfies their needs

Far from the "Tower of Flock", the sheep feed and drink
From the stream or wells with troughs that link
We tend them carefully through the day,
So none will be hurt, blemished, or stray

Shepherds of Bethlehem are we
Shepherds of our family trees
Living in the far fields near Bethlehem
Where the flocks graze each day
Eating the grass and hay

THIRSTY SHEEP

Anne

Anne is young and in love with Abel
She is sweet, warm, gentle, and kind … but determined
She wants to have children

ANNE:
My friend Rachel was most kind to let me come with her today
For I want to know what shepherds do
As they tend the sheep each day
I also want to be close to Abel, who I love in every way

It was three years ago that I knew
That Abel was sent by God to me
A man so kind, caring, and sincere too
A man that I could spend my life with, is he

As the years progressed we talked and laughed
To funny stories Abel just made up
Times that brought him closer to my heart
Praying each day we would never part

As the years quickly grew
Our closeness became to where it was just us
At all family gatherings held anew,
With family praying that our marriage would soon be thus

But because many citizens considered shepherds
As dishonest, lazy, unclean sinners, and outcasts,
Papa still had reservations

FAMILY GATHERING

19

ANNE (CONT'D):

But, Papa never saw these faults in Abel in all his observations

In truth, Abel was liked by everyone
Children loved to play games with him cause they always won
And, on occasion, Papa would join in Abel's conversations too
To find him agreeable to all his points of view

Despite my age, and that I am Papa's only child
Papa still considers me his precious little girl
From experience, I know, I can turn Papa's grin into a smile
For me, it takes just a little while

And so Papa decreed that he would make his decision soon
Whether our engagement could commence in just a few moons
And a marriage that could then be formally planned
By giving Abel his blessing and my hand

PAPA TOBIAS

CHILDREN WANTING TO SEE ABEL

THE CHILDREN LOVE ABEL

Moses

NARRATOR:
Moses is not a Temple shepherd, he tends the sheep of his Uncle Jethro
Moses is a historian who tends sheep on a field close to the Temple fields
He understands well what must be done to keep the sheep properly cared for
He is quiet, observant, and good natured

MOSES:
Not all of the lands near Bethlehem are priestly lots
For, by law, some plots must be for others
Jacob, Rachel's father, and Jethro own some of those spots
I am a shepherd too, like my Temple brothers

In Summer there are many hot and humid days,
Where sheep become stressed and painful
So Jacob's sons, who are with him today
Will help shear their sheep to keep those feelings away

Later, Jacob's sons will help me do the same
With Jethro's sheep that I tend
For fleecing is not a job for any one man
Large flocks like Jethro's require many volunteered hands

Shepherds that are not those of the Temple priests
Tend many more sheep compared to theirs
But they too will rest their sheep near the Temple folds
For safety increases with more guards there

SHEARS

WOOL

21

Abel about to begin a new work day

ABEL:
Oh, what a beautiful morning! No fog, just a lot of light!
I don't know if I ever saw the sun ever so big and bright
The skies are a deep sky blue with clouds plenty white
The dew is still on the ground with just a little breeze
The birds are chirping steadily in the tall trees

Come Abraham, Lot, Mesha, and others
Awake from your night's sleep
It is time now to start a new day
For we have many sheep to keep

This morning looks to be a great day
Calm and beautiful, a delightful treat
Plenty of rainwater for the sheep to drink
And safe wild greens for them to eat

Attend first to your daily needs
Then partake of your food right away
We'll meet shortly at the fold
There we'll pray to start our new day

Now that everyone has gathered near
Let us recite our prayers with Abraham here
That God will keep our sheep and us safe today
From any harm that may come our way

BIRDS CHIRPING

THE START OF A NEW DAY

22

ABEL (CONT'D):
Evening will come in ten short hours
So, let us not be fools
For the Temple flocks must be grazed and watched
According to the priest's strict rules

Abraham

Abraham is the most religious of all of the shepherds
He could have been a priest had he not liked shepherding so much
He leads all of the Temple shepherds in daily prayers

ABRAHAM AND ALL OF THE SHEPHERDS:
Father, we pray for all those in need,
For all our friends and families
We pray for your wisdom to see them through
When life is hard and good times few

Please keep our parents in your heart
Our siblings too, each day
Guide them so they will never part
May they pray for us, as we, they

Though our families are often far from sight
They are never far from our minds
Keep them all from any harm
As they labor on the family farm

We also pray for relatives and friends
Who have at times, passed away
May they too share in your eternal reward,
To live with you our Lord

Finally, when age makes it time for us to rest
May we also be so blessed,
To be able to share Heaven with you,
And with all those you chose too

Amen

End of Act 1, Scene 1

Act 1, Scene 2 – The Work Day

Moses, normally a very quiet person, joins in the shepherds' soliloquy with great passion

MOSES:
We are Bethlehem shepherds and happy to be
Just 80 miles south of the Sea of Galilee
Rising each morning to each new day
Tending our sheep carefully in every way
Knowing God is always on our side, we pray

Heat, wind, rain, and cold
Won't keep us from doing the work that we know
They will not keep us from our goal
To care for and protect the sheep we control

For we were born to be shepherds and free
That is what God wanted us to be

A shepherd's work is not easy
As we strive to cope with a steady hand
Each day brings forth a new beginning,
To do our best on the grazing land

For we were born to be shepherds and free
That is what God wanted us to be

And, though we are not rich in wealth,
We do our best to maintain our faith and health
For together they provide the foundation of oneself
The very thing our Lord would want himself

For we were born to be shepherds and free
That is what God wanted us to be

**THE SHEPHERDS ARE SURPRISED BY
MOSES' OUTBURST**

Abel takes command of the shepherds to start the day's efforts

ABEL:

With our prayers now done
Let us call our sheep today
It is Abraham's turn to be the first this morning
For he was the last to call yesterday

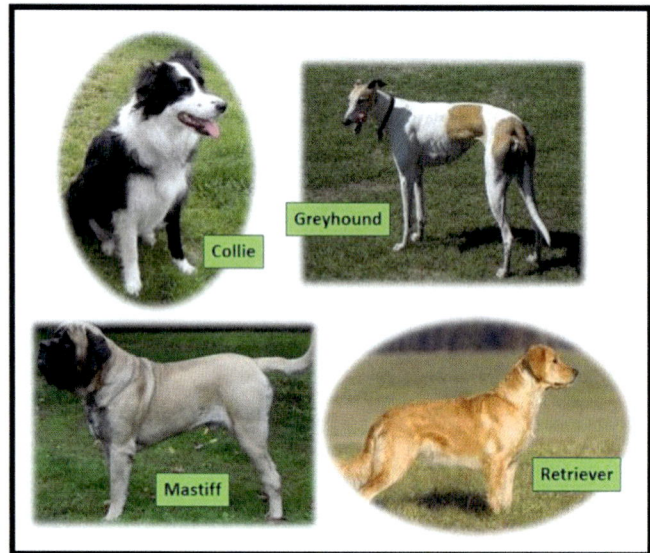

NARRATOR:

The new day begins

When Abraham's call engulfed the fold
Only his dog and ewes accepted his voice
They, in turn, bleated to their lambs
Told to follow the dog's movements to the new grazing expanse
Assigned to Abraham last night by a friendly game of chance

Sheepdogs are trained to keep the sheep controlled,
To herd the sheep to them, to pastures, or folds
Collies, Mastiffs, Greyhounds, and Retrievers are quite bold
These are just a few of the breeds used during times of old

Though sheep are often much larger
And just as fast as the dogs themselves,
A dog's ability to herd the sheep excels
Because sheep do not view dogs as friends
That is why they will run from what frightens them
Even though the dogs will protect them to the end

Soon commands could be heard
As Abraham called his dog Silas to gather his sheep
"Get Up", "Come By", and "Steady", were some of the words
Silas needed to control the sheep by executing various turns and curves
All of this Silas accomplished successfully
Without spooking or stressing the herd

NARRATOR:
Abel decides when to call the next shepherd in the queue

ABEL:
It is now time for Lot to do the same
Given that Abraham and his dog Silas had done their chores
And for all the other shepherds to follow the last
According to the order decided upon before

All of the flocks have now been led
To good pasture lands and water
We must now perform the duties
For which we had been ordered

SILAS HEEDS ABRAHAM'S CALLS TO CONTROL THE SHEEP

Isaac

NARRATOR:
Isaac is a non-Temple shepherd who knows his job well and works hard to support his family

ISAAC:
Feeding, grooming, and protecting the sheep
Were some of our day's chores
Birthing new lambs, teaching sheep to stay together
And helping them to cross streams were more

We shepherds are busy all the day
Averting sheep from poisonous plants
Keeping them spotless from the clay,
As well as free from the ants

Putting olive oil on thorn scratches
Searching for lost ones that strayed
Moving sheep to other patches
Where there is green grass or hay

Lifting water from a well with a bucket and a rope
Where there were no pools of water on the slope
Cutting branches of leaves and twigs for them to eat
Finding pools of slow water to beat the heat

All of these tasks and more we did today,
In order for us to earn our pay

LOOKING FOR
THE LOST LAMB

LAMB FOUND

SHEEP WITH HORNS

Anne reminiscing about the day's events

ANNE:
What a beautiful morning this has been
The clouds so white and skies so blue
With Rachel mentoring me always with slight grins,
As we tend her father's sheep through and through

I am so blessed to have a friend like her,
Who continues to watch over my life
Helping me whenever my needs appear
And encouraging Papa often to let me be Abel's wife

But little did I know today, that Rachel also made plans
For me to join Abel in but a short time
With food, she made for us with her skilled hands,
Fresh breads and cheeses made with olives, figs, dates, and wine

A large cloth to lay our food upon, Rachel also brought
And a mantle for me for any cold breeze that may come our way
Just Abel and Anne alone, Rachel thought,
Just Abel and Anne, no better pair than they

MOM & DAD

CHEESES WITH OLIVES, FIGS, DATES, AND WINE

SWEETHEARTS

MANTLE

RACHEL

BREADS

WINE

LARGE CLOTH

29

ANNE (CONT'D):
It was not long after Rachel left me
That Abel arrived with a startled glance
Pretending, with arms outstretched, and a smirk on his face
That our meeting was just a happenstance

I'm sure that was Rachel's doing as well
Who knew Abel would play the part
Since she had seen him many times before
Telling me funny stories just to warm my heart

Soon plenty of thoughts raced through our minds
That we felt we needed to share this day
Marriage, children, and our life thereafter
Helpful matters should Papa say
That our marriage would be OK

Then, as we sat, laughing and talking
And dreaming of our wishful marriage day
We ate the meal Rachel had prepared
Spread out on the beautiful linen cloth she had made

Oh Rachel, thank you for this delightful treat
Truly, a friend that is so sweet
Abel and I love you dearly
And so does God, so sincerely

SWEETHEARTS

NARRATOR:

The 10-hour work day is over
Time now to rest for the night and to organize the nightly guard watches
The sheep folds and the shepherds' hut for sleeping are close to one another
Shepherds take turns sleeping based on their nightly watches

ABEL:

The day has been long and the sheep are now fed
The sky is beginning to darken, so we need to get to bed
So let us return the sheep to the folds,
According to the order soon to be told

It is time now for us to rest this night,
For we are all weary from this day's play
Knowing tomorrow may not be so bright,
As it was so beautiful today

Now that the sheep are all in the folds,
Laban and Amos, it is your turn
To take the first of the two-hour watches tonight
Make sure the fires will continue to burn
To keep the wild beasts out of sight

Shepherds that are not on guard tonight
Will now go home and return tomorrow
With food and drink for our day's delight
For each day we do this borrow

**SHEPHERD'S HUT FOR
SLEEPING NEAR THE FOLDS**

DARKNESS APPROACHING

AMOS   LABAN

Amos, Laban, Lot & Mesha

NARRATOR:

Amos and Laban are a good team that perform their tasks dutifully
So too are Mesha and Lot
Lot is a strapping young man with a rebellious attitude
He is boisterous and crusty with a warm heart
He is the ultimate protector

AMOS:

We watched the folds with Anne during our 2-hour watch
And all was quiet as a mouse
It is time now for others to take our place
So Laban, call the next guards from the house

LABAN:

Mesha and Lot arise from your deep sleep
It is your turn now to watch the sheep
Amos and I need some rest
So, please get up to do your best

LOT:

Mesha sensed the four wolves nearby
Lurking close to the folds for a sheep-kill
But we with our staffs and slings
Got them to retreat uphill

All is quiet again in the folds
So we will continue our watch

AMOS

LABAN

LOT

MESHA

WOLF PACK GETTING READY TO ATTACK !

SHEEPFOLD

NARRATOR:
Anne reflecting on what she had learned today

ANNE:
Rachel is a courageous woman throughout,
Who graciously took me under her wing
To show me what shepherding is all about
I've learned so much today I could sing

Rachel cares greatly for the sheep she tends
With a desire to teach what she knows to all friends
Who enjoys seeing good things happen to those she cares about
Highly respected by her peers and dearly loved by Jacob, no doubt

Today I have seen what shepherds really do
And found what people say about shepherds is totally untrue
As I have clearly seen there is no free time each day
For sheep are like young children that get into trouble every which way

Unlike the days of King David,
Shepherds are now despised in everyday life
They are considered second-class and unworthy
And deprived of all civil rights

But, if Abel wants to take these untruths and place them aside
After his days with the Temple priests are over
Then Abel will indeed remain a shepherd for the rest of his life
With me standing by him, his loving wife

We'll raise a happy family of at least a few
And when our children have grown
They too will become shepherds with sheep of their own
Yes, we'll be shepherds, the best ever known

That is, if Papa would only give Abel his blessing!

ANNE HOPING

**SHE PRAYS DAILY
THAT HER FUTURE
WILL BE THUS**

PAPA
TOBIAS

YES

YES

YES

YES

SHEEP

CHILDREN

ANNE'S PRAYERS

- PAPA WILL ACCEPT ABEL
- ABEL MARRIES ANNE
- THEY WILL HAVE CHILDREN
- THE FAMILY WILL BE SHEPHERDS

Papa Tobias

NARRATOR:

Papa is in a quandary about Anne's future with someone other than himself

PAPA TOBIAS:

My God, my God, please help me to decide
Which man should I give my daughter to as his bride
Please God, help me to make the right choice
So that all in my family will come to rejoice

Anne, my daughter, one so loving and kind
May her love never fade from her Mother and me
A bond I assumed would stand the test of time
As long as we were a family of three

Why it seems like only yesterday
That I cradled her each day in my arms
And watched her sleep in the bed I had made
From cherished olive trees on our farm

And, through the years I saw her mature
Into a beautiful young lady of grace
But, even then, she always had a desire
For her Papa to hold her in his embrace

But, now I must choose the right man

That would love and treat Anne with respect
One that would care for her and provide
A man whose family would never be one of neglect
Truly, one that Anne could accept with great pride

Over the years, many wealthy men had wished for her hand
But none were shepherds, like Abel, that worked our lands
My God, my God, please help me to decide
Is Abel the one to forever be by her side?

End of Act 1, Scene 2

Act 2, Scene 3 – Shepherd's Faith Tested

ST. LUKE

Chapter 2
Verses 1-9

NARRATOR:

"Now it came to pass in those days, that a decree went forth from Caesar Augustus that a census of the whole world should be taken and all were going, each to his own town, to register"

"And Joseph also went from Galilee, out of the town of Nazareth into Judea to the town of David, which is called Bethlehem – because he was of the House and Family of David – to register, together with Mary his espoused wife, who was with child"

"And it came to pass while they were there, that the days for her to be delivered were fulfilled and she brought forth her firstborn son, and wrapped him in swaddling clothes, and laid him in a manger; because there was no room for them in the inn"

"And there were shepherds in the same district living in the fields and keeping watch over their flock by night"

Jesus is Born in Bethlehem

**NAZARETH TO BETHLEHEM
DISTANCE = 70.5 AIR MILES,
OR ABOUT 80 ROAD MILES**

**BETHLEHEM
BY VASILY DMITRIEVICH POLENOV, 1882**

*Thanks
be to God!*

An Angel Appears to the Bethlehem Shepherds

NARRATOR:

But, just then, all of the shepherds in Bethlehem were startled

Suddenly, an angel of the Lord stood by them and the glory of God shone around them, and they feared exceedingly

And the angel said to them

ANGEL:

"Do not be afraid, for behold, I bring you good news of great joy which shall be to all the people;

For today in the Town of David, a Savior has been born to you, who is Christ the Lord

And, this shall be a sign to you: you shall find an infant wrapped in swaddling clothes lying in a manger."

ST. LUKE

Chapter 2
Verses 8-13

NARRATOR:

All of the shepherds begin to question what they have seen and heard
They need to decide what they should do about it
Jacob, Abel, and Isaac have their say

JACOB:

All of us had seen the angel and heard him say
That a Savior was born in Bethlehem today
Thus, I will talk to Abel to ease our fright
Perhaps together we can shed some light
On what had been seen by all the shepherds tonight

ABEL:

Who is this child that we must go
To pay homage to him? Born this very day
In this Town of David
A town, not far away

Why is this child so different from others?
Why must we go to see him?
That we do not know where
Without family or friends, to travel there

Why must we go to see a child,
Who we do not know, for even a while?
With no food or gifts to give;
To him, where he was born
To him, where he now lives

ABEL (CONT'D):

Indeed, who is this child, that we must go our way
To pay homage to him, born this very day
On this cold, and silent night,
Lying in a manger, bathed in starlight

But! Could it be that this child is the Savior, foretold to come;
To save the world from all its sins?
And that tonight the child was really born in Bethlehem;
And, we must follow this star to him

Could it be that God has chosen us to be the first
To see this child, this cold and starry night?
Wrapped in swaddling clothes,
Lying in a manger, bathed in starlight

But why were we chosen, poor shepherds of the fields?
Not of royalty are we
That God would pick us without armor or shields
To see this child this eve

Surely the Temple priests will not be pleased
Should we fail to execute their defined tasks,
To keep their sheep spotless and from all harm
For these sheep are needed for their religious acts

Our families too will incur Temple rage
For they too rely on our wages
To help supplement their way of life,
To provide food and clothing for our siblings of all ages

SHEPHERDS CONFERRING ON WHAT
TO MAKE OF THE
ANGEL'S ANNOUNCEMENT

ABEL (CONT'D):

Thus, to help me to decide
I will confer with Jacob who is most wise
Together we will assess what we will do
That is best for us and you

ISAAC:

We need to make a decision soon
For the sun is beginning to cease
The longer that decision takes
The travel danger will increase

As one can clearly see
The evening light is beginning to dim
Soon the sun will disappear
Then darkness and shadows on objects will appear
These are the very things sheep fear

Thus, should we go to Bethlehem,
We must indeed go now and slow,
So as not to alarm the sheep,
Carrying a torch ahead that glows

There are hundreds of sheep in the fold
Too many to bring and control
So, if we decide to go tonight
We must select what sheep we'll take
Not just for the child but for our very own sake

ISAAC:
We must decide then too
As to which shepherds will go, and those who will stay
For we cannot leave the folds unguarded
From the wild beasts and robbers that are cold hearted

NARRATOR:
Abraham is the exception - he need not question anything.
God had given us a message.

ABRAHAM:
I, Abraham for one, do believe
That the angel's message is real
That we are to go to Bethlehem to see the child this eve
Perhaps there is more there for his family to reveal

Why we were chosen, I do not care
Our Lord has summoned us, please do not despair
We must do his will as he commands
That is all one needs to understand

Let us go to Bethlehem today
Without further deliberation
Time is fleeting, we must be on our way
We need to put aside any more consideration

NARRATOR:
However, Moses, who is not as religious as Abraham, still has doubts

MOSES:
How do we know that this apparition
Is not from our Lord?
But rather a cunning plan of the Devil,
That we should carefully ignore

Surely for us to take this more seriously
There must be more proof
That God did indeed send us this message
That we should follow through

Only then, will I accept
What I have seen and heard tonight
For ...

- FOR YOU TO DOUBT GOD
- LIVE IN FEAR
- FEEL INSECURE
- SKIP CHURCH
- BE LED ASTRAY
- FAIL

NARRATOR:
To Moses' indecision came a quick and overwhelming response

DEVIL'S PLAN

Many Angels Appear to the Bethlehem Shepherds

ST. LUKE

Chapter 2
Verses 13-14

NARRATOR:
Suddenly there was with the angel a multitude of the Heavenly Host praising God and saying,

"Glory to God in the highest, and on Earth peace among men of goodwill"

End of Act 2, Scene 3

Act 2, Scene 4 – Decisions & Journey

NARRATOR:
It is time now for all to make a decision on what to do
Abel with Jacob's help decides what is the best for all

ABEL:
All of the questions and concerns that we've had
Have now been answered by this added vision
So let us not question the events any further
As your guide and our friend Jacob too, this is our decision

Based on all of the heavenly events
That we have seen and heard this day
Our advice to you is this:
"Let us be quickly be on our way"

My sheep, they listen to my voice
Likewise, yours do the same
We call them, and they follow by choice
To each shepherd, who calls their name

But, if each of us brought several sheep on the road tonight
It will be difficult to control in the waning sunlight
So, we will bring just ten sheep from my fold,
For the parents and child to behold

The sheep we bring will be our gifts
To provide food and clothing for the Babe
Who, in time, will take his place
In the world of sin to save

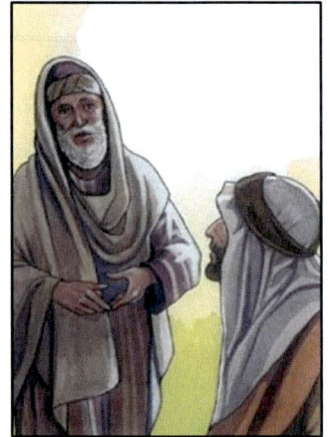

JACOB AND ABEL DISCUSS THE SPECIFICS OF A WORKABLE PLAN

SOME THINGS WE CONSIDERED

- WHO WILL GO
- WHEN WILL WE LEAVE
- WHO WILL WATCH THE FOLDS
- HOW MANY SHEEP WILL WE BRING
- WHOSE SHEEP
- WILL WE REST ALONG THE WAY
- WHAT WILL OUR FAMILIES THINK WHEN WE DON'T RETURN TONIGHT
- IT WILL BE DIFFICULT IN LITTLE LIGHT AND NARROW DIRT ROADS WITH STONES
- ETC.

ABEL (CONT'D):

We will not fear what the Temple priests will say
When they learn that we left this day
And gave a few of their sheep to an infant not far away
That was lying in a manger of hay

For the angel told us that he is the Savior, that was foretold to come
To save the world from all its sins;
For tonight the Christ Child was born in Bethlehem
And, we must follow this star to him
To be the first to see this holy child, this cold and starry night
Lying in a manger, bathed in starlight

Abraham, Isaac, Jacob, Rachel, and my dog Ada
Will make the journey with me without delay
For the child is waiting for us this day

Since Anne is with Rachel, she will come too
But Anne's father must be told so he will not fear
That Anne did not return home when she was due,
Fearing something bad had happened to her here

So, take your staffs and slings for us to be on our way
Let us go to Bethlehem before the day's light is away

David, Moses, Job, Doeg, and two others
Will keep watch over the rest of the sheep
While we go to Bethlehem
To find the child we seek

ABEL (CONT'D):
Come now my sheep follow me
Do not be timid or flee
Listen to your mother's bleat
As she calls you to meet
Follow her as she moves to the star's light
That shines on Bethlehem this very night

NARRATOR:
Despite Lot having full trust in all of Abel's expert advice and decisions, he now questions this

LOT:
Abel and Jacob have decided which shepherds will go
On what basis I do not know
Whereas Abel, a Temple shepherd, is the wisest and oldest
I am the youngest, strongest, and boldest

I can provide us with protection
From any danger that might occur
Also, there are plenty of others
To watch over the sheep and one another

I OBJECT!

But most of all, I too
Would like to see the child
That was revealed to us this night
Please know that what I say is true
So Abel would it be alright?

NARRATOR:
Following Lot's lead, Mesha also voices his concern about Abel's decision

MESHA:
I too question Abel's choices
If Lot can go, then I want to go too
For Lot and I are a team
That watch the sheep each night anew

ME TOO!

MESHA (CONT'D):
From animals and persons that are mean

Our past experience has shown
That we are most capable
For we have not lost even a single sheep
To wild beasts or robbers that were able

So please Abel, let us both be allowed to go with thee
All will be glad we did
For we'll do our best on the road to please
To keep everyone's mind at ease

LOT'S AND MESHA'S ADVICE TO ALL THOSE THAT DARE TO ENTER THE SHEEPFOLDS

ELSE YOU WILL FEEL MUCH PAIN !!!

STOP
DO NOT ENTER

ROBBERS
JACKAL
LION
BEAR
WOLF
HYENA

Having heard and processed Lot's and Mesha's complaint, Abel allows them to go too

ABEL:
Yes Lot and Mesha, your points are quite right
So both of you will go with us tonight

Our journey will take but just a little while
For Bethlehem is not too far, just a few miles
To travel in almost no light
To where our Savior resides this night

Come my sheep, let us leave this place
To begin our journey to Bethlehem
To see the manger filled with grace
The child and the rest of them

Do not be worry about the downhill and darkness
Or shadows that may change by whim
For tonight the child was born in Bethlehem;
And, we must follow this star to him

ABEL LEADS THE SHEEP SO THEY WILL NOT BE FRIGHTENED

Rachel makes a last minute request of Abel

RACHEL:
Yes, we must hurry, the time is tight
Soon there will be little light
The wind has begun to take flight
And rain is just hours from our sight

Please Abel, would it be alright
To take a little time to let my family know
Of the angels and why we must go tonight
And why they must now help tend our sheep so

If we can pause for just a short while
Anne's parents and all others will be made aware
That something wonderful happened this day
And that everyone is safe in our care

The road to Bethlehem goes by our farm
Halfway to our goal
There we will rest, protected from harm,
For sleep is needed for our souls

And while we let our families know
I would like to bring some gifts besides
Swaddling clothes, shawls, and carry bags
Items to express my family's love and pride

JACOB'S FARM
(HOUSE AND BARN)

RACHEL (CONT'D):

The gifts will not cause much of a delay
For all these items had long been stored away
My children have all grown old with young adults of their own
They have no need for these today

The swaddling clothes are made of fine linen
Long strips to wrap the baby's arms, legs, and chest
The clothes will provide the baby with a happy disposition
Feeling as though he is in his mother's caress

Unlike the clothes, the shawls are made of fine wool
While the carry bags are made of leather
The shawls will wrap the baby about his body
I will bring two to protect the baby from the weather

So please Abel, give us a little time while we are on our way
It will not cause much of a delay
To see the child as the angel said
Lying in the manger of hay

End of Act 3, Scene 4

Act 3, Scene 5 – The Visitation

NARRATOR:
Abel decides to allow the group to rest before moving on to Bethlehem

ABEL:
The sheep are sleepy, in need of rest
For the path is difficult at best
So we will stop at Jacob's farm to reduce the stress
To keep us warm we will build a fire
From kindling we find in the nearby mire

So my sheep, stay by me
For it is night time you see
The winds are mild for you my sheep,
Safe for you to fall asleep

Carefully lay your chins upon the ground
Try not to make any sound
As always, I will guard you as you lay
Later we will continue on our way
To find the child that was foretold
By the angels and prophets of old

An hour of rest is all we'll need
To complete our journey with little speed
So my sheep do pay heed
When I call you again by name to follow me

Abel decides to continue the trip

ABEL:
We have now rested
Let us begin the journey anew

Rise now everyone, the time appears
For us to again to be on our way
For Bethlehem, is where we must be this day
To find the child, lying in a manger
Probably guarded by angels from all danger

That right my sheep, follow me
Down the road to the town's gate
There to find the child by God's decree
The search according to our fate

Isaac makes a point that had not been addressed before

We do not know the hour the child was born today
And, if the family will be sleeping when we arrive
So, it is by fate, that we must accept, what the angel did say
That the family will greet us without trepidation or delay

EWE WITH HER TWINS

NARRATOR:
Rachel quickly counters Isaac's statement

RACHEL:
Isaac, place trust in what you have seen and heard
We have been given God's word

Oh Isaac, please don't worry or be upset
For the angel told us not to fret
I'm sure the family will be wide awake
Waiting for our arrival, no mistake

Anne and I are most anxious to see the child tonight
To touch his hands and hold him tight
To see his eyes open wide with great delight
To see his chubby arms and legs take flight
To see his parents so forthright

To tell them of heavenly sights
And to wish them a blessed good night
Only then will this holy night seem right

Rachel's excitement grows as the group neared Bethlehem
However, she and the group anticipated what would happen when they arrived

RACHEL:

We are almost there!
Just a short distance to the gate
Here are some other things to consider
Before it becomes too late

OLIVE TREES IN SHEPHERD'S FIELD NEAR BETHLEHEM

NARRATOR:

As they walked along the road
All discussed what they would say
To the child's parents while he lay
On this very hopeful day

They too were uncertain as to how long they could stay
Before the sun would begin to rise the next day
For they knew the family would need to rest
That the child would need to feed from the breast

But what they pondered most of all
Is what they would see when they got to the stall
For they had seen plenty of infants before
How would this child be so different?
A child they would ultimately adore.

Perhaps they would see him bathed in light,
With a halo around his head,
Or would they see angels protecting him instead

They wondered too if his parents would be alarmed
When they arrived this night unannounced
That the family might think they're there to do them harm,
Or would they welcome them with open arms

All these things and more they questioned
But none for which they could immediately solve
Thus, only when they reached the stall
Would these issues be finally resolved

**ANSWERS ARE BUT
A SHORT DISTANCE AWAY**

BETHLEHEM

Anne is overwhelmed by the days events

ANNE:
Oh Rachel, what a lovely day this has been
With clear blue skies, and just the right amount of heat
From a beautiful morning's start to a glorious day's end
And two heavenly events to soon make our day complete

If I had not been with you this very day
I would not have seen the angels that came our way
To give us the good news that our Savior was born this very night
To tell us that we must go to see Him without hesitation or fright

I'm sure you too heard the angel say
That God will give us a sign
That will let us know where to find the child
A Savior, conceived by God's design

When I pray for the child and his parents
I too would like to say a prayer
For God to help Papa to decide
To let me become Abel's bride
In time to a marriage, full of love and pride

And, while I know that my leaving him
Will make Papa feel lonely and sad
I know his sadness will quickly turn to one of joy
As soon as we have children for him to adore

NARRATOR
Abraham proudly announces that their journey has come to a successful end

ABRAHAM
The angel's messages have been fulfilled, we are here
After searching Bethlehem, in the wind and the rain, for quite some time
We found the child lying in a manger with Mary and Joseph at his side
With a fire warming the stall from outside

ANNE AND THE SHEPHERDS VISITING THE HOLY FAMILY

NARRATOR:

It was surprising to find upon entering the stall
That the parents quickly welcomed them all
An indication that they had been heavenly pre-told
That the shepherds would visit, despite the rain and cold

But, as they knelt to pay homage to the child
They saw an infant like those they had cared for before
A child they had held on bended knees and adored

They saw no halo, or angels, to protect the child
Nor could the child stand by himself for even a while
No, a baby, they surmised, no different than they had seen before
A baby they had cuddled often on chests and more

But, though he was as beautiful as others before
They soon found him much different from those that came before
For here was an alert, calm, and peaceful child
With eyes widely opened as he smiled

Whose face focused greatly on Mary's sounds
One looking to greet everyone around
Truly a gifted child, so profound

All of these remarkable characteristics and more they saw during their stay
Convinced the shepherds that their Savior was indeed born this day

BABY JESUS – OUR SAVIOR!

NARRATOR:

Just then Rachel, a lovely woman with a heart so true
Asked Mary if she could touch the infant for just a second or two
And, perhaps hold and hug him too
Oh, joy!
Mary a woman so kind and dear, as any were
Carefully handled the child to her

As Rachel held the child close to her breasts
Anne placed her shawl upon the child's back
To keep the child warm as he rests
A show of Anne's love and devotion that he would never lack

And, as Rachel softly cradled his head
The child happily settled in bed
But as he slept, his mouth appeared beaming
Making everyone wondering what he was dreaming

It was then that Abel assigned Isaac to tell the parents of the heavenly events
On how they were chosen to be the first to see the Child
The Savior that would save the world from all its sins
During his talk, Mary silently took this all within

Just then the star grew very bright
As the Child lifted his arms with great delight
To the heavens, they rose on high
To proclaim to the world with a loving rapport
What the prophet Isaiah foretold centuries before

ISAIAH

Chapter 9

Verse 6

"For a Child will be born to us, a Son will be given to us;

And, the authority will rest on His shoulders;

And his name will be called Wonderful Counselor, Mighty God, Eternal Father, Prince of Peace"

End of Act 3, Scene 5

Act 3, Scene 6 – The Message

NARRATOR:
After spending some time with the family, Abel decides it is time to leave and return home

ABEL:
With the sun slowly rising in the east
I see that the light in Bethlehem has increased
Urging us to be on our way
So let us return home to tell the Temple priests
For the family needs to rest this day

NARRATOR:

It was then that Joseph called the sheep
The name Abel gave to him
Miraculously they came without a peep
And laid down beside Joseph again

The clothes and sheep they brought, the shepherds gave
To the family to keep and raise
A reminder of their visit that night
Of their true devotion and praise

And though they knew the sheep they gave
Were those bred for Temple worship,
They did not know that the Child one day
Would die for their sins and they would pray

Gifts of
swaddling clothes
and carry bags

BETHLEHEM
VISITORS
Their endless love
and devotion

Temple Sheep

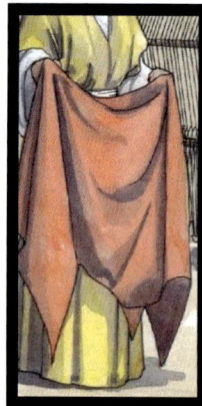

Mantles

Isaac, who had doubts before, is now most anxious to tell the world of this night's happenings

Abel, now a firm believer in the Christ Child, encourages Isaac to tell him the story he wishes to tell

ISAAC:
We need to tell the priests and the other shepherds too
Of the events that made us go astray
As well of the Temple sheep we gave away
To our Savior this day

To tell them of the angels' announcements last night
That caused us much fright
That told us that the Messiah was born in Bethlehem that night
And that he would be found wrapped in swaddling clothes
Lying in a manger, bathed in starlight

To tell them also what Mary told us
How an angel appeared to her and said thus
How she would give birth despite her being a maiden
For God had chosen her from all creation

That the Child was the Savior foretold to come,
To save the world from all its sins
And that we had been chosen by God to become
The very first to go to Bethlehem to see Him

NARRATOR:
Abel assigns Isaac to inform the priests and the other shepherds

But, surprisingly, to all of Isaac's words, the Temple priests just smiled with a grin and the High Priest said

HIGH PRIEST:
We believe all the events you have told us today
That our Savior's birth did occur that way
What you did to see the Child, we very much agree
And, the sheep you gave were indeed appropriate for the family of three
Now we must tell the world of this heavenly event
To all the ends of the earth is our intent
Without delay, the word of our Savior's birth must be sent

NARRATOR:
Just then, all of the priests smiled again and the High Priest said to Abel and Anne

ISAAC INFORMING THE PRIESTS OF THE DAY'S EVENTS

HIGH PRIEST:
We want you to know that Tobias had come to see us early this day
To tell us that he had decided to let your marriage proceed this way
A wedding that will occur just two months away
Thus, let us all rejoice for what has transpired today

So, Abel, hug and kiss Anne your future bride
For your engagement is now officially formalized

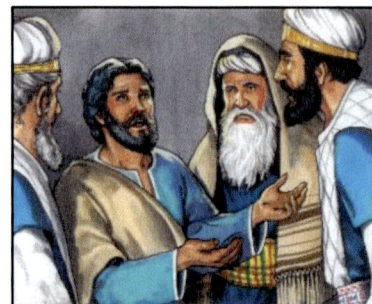

PRIESTS DISCUSSING WHAT ISAAC TOLD THEM

Hallelujah !!!

Our Savior has been born !!!

Glory be to God!

Wedding !!!

PAPA TOBIAS DECIDES TO LET
ABEL AND ANNE MARRY

NARRATOR:

Isaac's message of Jesus' birth filled all of the Bethlehem shepherds and villagers with feelings of great joy!

ISAAC

Isaac then said to them: "Let the message, that our Savior has been born, be sent to all the corners of the Earth!"

ISAAC

Anne said proudly at her wedding:
"Thanks be to God! Papa says our family will indeed be shepherds!"

Oh my!
Look at all the sheep Papa gave Abel and me as a wedding present!

For tonight, God chose to invite the lowest of the low
To celebrate the birth of his Son
Thus, we too, can have a relationship with Him
By each coming to Him as one

Yes, one and all everywhere,
Keep the Child in your daily prayer
And all the things we had heard and seen,
On this special night, so serene

Amen

End of Act 3, Scene 6

A Christmas Message From Jesus

If you look for me at Christmas

Poem Author: Jan Mahannah

If you look for me at Christmas,
you won't need a special star.
I'm no longer just in Bethlehem,
I'm right there where you are.
You may not be aware of me,
amid the celebrations.
You'll have to look beyond the stores,
and all the decorations.
But if you take a moment,
from your list of things to do,
and listen to your heart, you'll find
I'm waiting there for you.
You're the one I want to be with,
you're the reason that I came.
And you'll find me in the stillness,
as I'm whispering your name.

Love, Jesus

Life After Jesus' Birth

Anno Domini (AD): 1-12

Life After Jesus' Birth

The Holy Family Part 1 of 2

JOURNEY OF THE MAGI' WAS CREATED IN C.1894 BY JAMES TISSOT IN REALISM STYLE.

- Sometime after Jesus was born in Bethlehem of Judea in the days of King Herod, three wise men (Magi) came to Jerusalem saying "where is He that is born King of the Jews? For we had seen his star in the East and had come to worship Him." (Matthew 2: 1-3)

- Then, after the Jewish chief priests and scribes of the people searched the scriptures they told Herod and the Magi that a prophet had written that "From Bethlehem shall come forth a leader who shall rule my people Israel". (Matthew 2: 4-6).

- Upon seeing the Child with Mary his mother; the Magi fell to the ground and worshiped him. Then, "opening their treasures, they offered Him gifts of gold, frankincense, and myrrh.

- And, being warned in a dream to not return to Herod, the Magi went back to their country by another way". (Matthew 2: 10-12)

Life After Jesus' Birth

The Holy Family Part 2 of 2

JOURNEY OF THE MAGI' WAS CREATED IN C.1894 BY JAMES TISSOT IN REALISM STYLE.

- When the Magi had departed, an angel of the Lord appeared in a dream to Joseph telling him to flee to Egypt with Mary and the infant Jesus, for Herod will seek the Child to destroy him. The angel also said to "remain there until I tell thee". (Matthew: 2: 13)

- After King Herod had died, Joseph withdrew his family to the town of Nazareth in the region of Galilee. (Matthew 2: 15)

- And after they had performed all things according to the law of the Lord, they returned into Galilee, to their city Nazareth. And the Child grew, and became strong, full of wisdom; and the grace of God was in Him. (Luke 2: 39-40).

- At about age 30, Jesus left Nazareth to begin the ministry that God had predestined for Him. (Matthew 3: 13)

Life After Jesus' Birth

Abel & Anne

- After two years of marriage, Abel felt it was his time to retire as a Temple shepherd.

- During those two years, Anne tended the sheep Papa gave them on Jacob's land with Rachel's occasional help.

- Abel's relatives also helps Anne to tend the sheep whenever they could.

- Abel's family are all shepherds now, and like Jacob own hundreds of sheep on their own pasture land.

- Abel and Anne are as much in love today as they always were before marriage.

- Abel's and Anne's faith in God remains strong and their family often prays for Jesus, their relatives, and friends.

Life After Jesus' Birth

The children & their sheep dog

Jacob
Age 2

- Abel and Anne have 4 children (2 girls and 2 boys).

- The children love playing with and caring for the sheep each day.

- Abel continues to tell funny stories to make Anne and their children laugh.

- Mary, Joseph, and Rachel always listen attentively to their big brother.

- Emmanuel thought it cute to name the children's new dog after Jacob.

- He also taught Jacob the calls he needed to know in order to control the sheep.

- Jacob willingly accepts calls from all of the children and Anne, but not from Abel.

Anne laughingly tells the children Abel's dog Ada told Jacob not to heed Abel's calls.

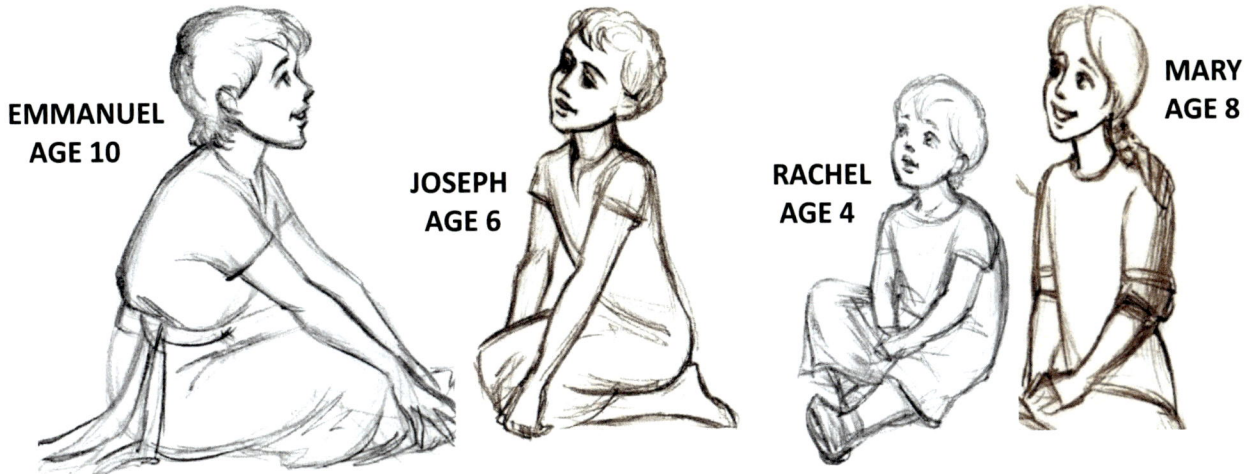

EMMANUEL
AGE 10

JOSEPH
AGE 6

RACHEL
AGE 4

MARY
AGE 8

Life After Jesus' Birth

Papa Tobias

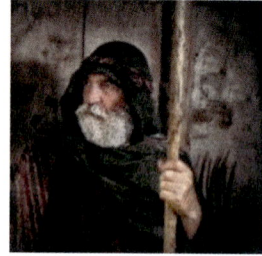

- Papa's wealthy friends also help Abel and Anne to tend their sheep. They found shepherding to be more comforting to their soul than dealing with their everyday activities of creating more wealth.

- Papa Tobias is always seen with a huge smile on his face whenever his grandchildren are around. He constantly makes excuses to be with them.

- Papa also helps to tend and shear the sheep whenever he can find time.

- He often says, he knows that God helped him to make the right decision to choose Abel for Anne.

- Papa also says that he wished he had been a shepherd himself, rather than a farmer.

Life After Jesus' Birth

Jacob & Rachel

- Jacob, Rachel, and their many sons continued to do what they had always done. After all, shepherding is in their blood.

- Jacob too gave Abel some of his sheep as a wedding present.

- Until Abel could acquire legal ownership of his own land, Jacob freely allowed Abel and Anne to tend their sheep on his pasture grounds.

- Jacob, Rachel, and their many sons also help Abel and Anne to shear their sheep each year.

- Jacob, Rachel, and Abel … no better mentors than they on all shepherding matters.

- Rachel and Jacob will soon celebrate their 60th wedding anniversary.

Life After Jesus' Birth

Abraham, Priests & Villagers

- Abraham decided, that regardless of age, he would always be a Temple shepherd, to be their religious brother. After all, that is what God had always wanted him to be.

- Having witnessed Abel's extended family over many years, the High Priest decided to set aside some special days of the year for shepherds to attend religious services.

- During those times, when the shepherds are at Mass, many members of the community volunteered to take turns tending their sheep.

- The High Priest, knowing that Abraham was very religious, and that he had wanted him to be a Priest rather than a shepherd, authorized him to be an Assistant Priest during these special services.

- The community, in which Abel and Anne live and they know well, continue to change their civil and religious views on shepherds for the better.

Life After Jesus' Birth

Isaac

Isaac, a non-Temple shepherd, had always tended sheep that were not his own. Sometimes he helped Jacob with his sheep.

- When Abel retired, his family had no younger sibling to take his place as a Temple shepherd.

- Therefore, upon consideration of Abel's, Jacob's, and the priests' suggestion, the High Priest chose Isaac to replace Abel.

- The added pay that Isaac now receives, as both a Temple shepherd and as their spokesperson and guide, became a Godsend to his family.

- Isaac continues to tell the story of Jesus' birth to all that he comes into contact with.

Life After Jesus' Birth

Moses and the Young Shepherds

- Moses continues to watch his Uncle Jethro's sheep and continues to keep close ties with Abel's family and his Temple brothers.

- The shepherds are often seen laughing as they hear Moses on many days singing loudly to the heavens.

- Actually, the sheep and his dog don't mind …. they are use to Moses' outbursts. They probably feel the noise helps to keep the wild beasts away.

- Lot, Mesha, Amos, and Laban are still very happy being Temple shepherds and close friends.

- They, and their dogs, continue to do their daily work with great responsibility and care.

- No wild animal or robber had ever harmed, or stolen, any of the Temple sheep during their watches.

LOT   MESHA   AMOS   LABAN

Life After Jesus' Birth

The Families

- Mama Tobias, Abel's mother, and Rachel love to make delicious treats for Abel and Anne's children.

- One would also see them, and Anne, scheming to create events just to get all of their families together for a good time.

- During those times and others, the women are always seen laughing and talking about everything.

- Their families continue to remain close to each other on all sorts of matters.

ABEL'S MOTHER  MAMA TOBIAS

 ANNE

 RACHEL

Contents

Acknowledgements

I would like to thank:

- Rev. Robert P. Hyde, Jr. and the late Deacon Donald R. Whiting of the Roman Catholic Diocese of Syracuse for their reviews of the very early manuscripts in 2020.

- Barry Vaughn of St. Margaret's Church in Mattydale, NY for his excellent review of the pre-final manuscript in January, 2022.

- Rev. Msgr. J. Robert Yeazel and Rev. John Manno of the Roman Catholic Diocese of Syracuse for their respective reviews of the play's manuscript in December, 2023 and February, 2024.

- Todd Hobin and Brett Hobin of the Hobin Studios for their friendship, musical knowledge, and their recordings of the many audio segments needed for the play.

- My family for their continued support throughout the development of the play.

Cast

Vocal Characters

Narrator: Denise (Colasanti) Munson

High Priest: David Munson

Lot: Liam Mahar

Abel: Richard Munson

Mesha: Aidan Mahar

Mary: Virginia Munson

Non-Vocal Characters

Moses: Daniel Colasanti, Jr.

Jacob: Timothy Mahar

Amos: Aidan Mahar

Isaac: Daniel Colasanti, Jr.

Jesus

Laban: Liam Mahar

Abraham: Timothy Mahar

Joseph

Angel Gabriel: Todd Hobin

Rachel: Mary Patricia (Colasanti) Mahar

Uncle Jethro

Anne: Gemma Margarita Colasanti

Moderator: Todd Hobin

Jacob's sons

Unnamed Shepherd: Denise (Colasanti) Munson

Sheep: Bleating Sounds

Children

Wolves: Growling Sounds

Foreword: Kimberly (McLaughlin) Colasanti

Family & Friends

Host of Angels: Denise (Colasanti) Munson

Closing Remark: Todd Hobin

Dogs: Ada, Silas, Noah & Jacob

Papa Tobias: Daniel Colasanti, Jr.

List of Artwork & Photos

Production

Audio Tracks and Musical Arrangements
Hobin Recording Studios

Todd Hobin
Recording artist, songwriter, producer, and studio musician
Email: todd@toddhobin.com
https://www.syracuse.com/entertainment/2014/01/todd_hobin_profile_syracuse_music.html

Brett Hobin – Studio Owner & Manager
brett@hobinstudios.com

8417 Oswego Rd. #192
Baldwinsville, NY 13027
Ph: (315) 622-0201

Todd Hobin Band
Booking Inquiries
John J. Pettigrass
Ph: (315) 412-2922

Artist Event Management
219 S. West Street, Suite 202
Syracuse, NY 13202
Email: johnjpettigrass@windstream.net

**The Hobin Studio audio tracks are utilized in the
PPT Flash Drives, Audiobook CDs, and DVDs**

Bibliography

Much of this play's imagination was developed from keywords found in countless online articles and books, as well as that derived from viewing religious illustrations. A partial list of them follows:

- http://www.Arielministries.org/ariel/roar_main_December2008.Html, *The real shepherds of Bethlehem*, by Nick Harris, December 2008

- https://www.Ancient-hebrew.org/manners/shepherd-life-the-care-of-sheep-and-goats.Htm, by Fred H. Wight, 1953

- Dr. Juergen Buehler, 22 Nov 2012, *The Tower of Flock*

- https://www.Jw.Org/en/library/magazines/wp20121101/the-shepherd/(Jehovah's Witnesses), *Life in Bible Times - The Shepherd*, 11/01/2012

- https://www.Biblestudytools.com/dictionary/shepherd/, *Shepherd*, Topics are from M.G. Easton M.A., D.D., Illustrated Bible Dictionary, Third Edition published by Thomas Nelson, 1897, public domain, copy freely

- https://www.Bible-history.Com/sketches/ancient/sheep-fold.Html, *Ancient Sheep Fold* (Bible history online)

- https://work.Chron.Com/duties-shepherd-23576.Html, *What are the duties of a shepherd*, by Beth Greenwood, updated June 28, 2018

- https://www.Chaimbentorah.Com/2014/12/hebrew-word-study-shepherds-%d7%a8%d7%a2%d7%99%d7%90/, *Hebrew Word Study – Shepherds* by Chaim & Laura, Dec 24, 2014

- http://bibleresources.Americanbible.org/resource/shepherds, *American Bible Society – resources*

- https://www.Gotquestions.Org/shepherd-in-the-bible.Html, *What was a shepherd in the Bible*

- http://powerofhumility.Org/migdal-eder, *Lamb of God - The Manger in Migdal Eder*, by Clairborne Mize, December 25, 2014

- http://www.Veganpeace.Com/animal_facts/sheep.Html

Bibliography (Cont'd)

- http://www.Btwol.Com/09_bible_study/06-bible-study-pdf/books/why%20the%20shepherd.Htm, *Why the Shepherd*, by Godfrey Bowan

- https://answers.Yahoo.Com/question/index, *Who Were Some Famous Biblical Shepherds?* – Anonymous asked in society & culture religion & spirituality · 1 decade ago

- https://www.Gotquestions.Org/high-priest.Html

- ttps://www.Biblestudy.Org/bible-study-by-topic/gemstones-in-the-bible/precious-stones-in-the-breastplate.Html, *High Priest Breastplate Gems - Bible Study*

- www.GNPI.org, Mr. Thomas Nutt, Vice President of Operations, Strategic Evangelism, Good News Production International and College Press Publishing Co., Bible story artwork by artist: Paula Nash Giltner: Illustrations

- https://search.Yahoo.Com/search?P=6-things-satan-wants-for-your-life&fr=yfp-t&fp=1&toggle=1&cop=mss&ei=utf-8

The following book provided the religious text relating to Jesus' birth.

- The Holy Bible … New American Catholic Edition, Benziger Brothers, Inc. © 1950, 1958

Special Thanks

Artwork and sound effects by permission of:

- **Mr. David Padfield,** https://www.Padfield.Com: **photos**

- **Mr. Paul Thompson,** www.Freebibleimages.Org: **illustrations**

- **Mr. Thomas Nutt, Vice President of Operations, Strategic Evangelism, Good News Production International and College Press Publishing Co., Bible story artwork by artist: Paula Nash Giltner: Illustrations**

- **Dr. Nicole Tilford, Society of Biblical Literature,** https://www.Sbl-site.org: **maps**

- ://www.Freesoundslibrary.com: **sound effect: sheep**

- **Mr. Don Lee, President of Horizons [companies],** https://horizonscompanies.com, **and artists John Morgan and Dave Fullen for their musical arrangement "What Child is This"**

Note: in addition to the gratuitous artwork mentioned above, many pieces of artwork were also purchased from Shutterstock.com for the play's commercial use.

About the Author

Daniel R. Colasanti, Sr.

Syracuse University

Syracuse, New York

BSEE (1964), MSEE (1972)

Graduate of General Electric's (GE's) Advanced Course in Engineering (ACE) program (1968-1972)

Dan is an experienced computer programmer, Sonar Systems Engineer, and Engineering Project Manager (EPM), having worked for General Electric (GE), Martin Marietta, Lockheed Martin, and the Sensis Corporation.

At GE, Martin Marietta, and Lockheed Martin, Dan worked primarily on Sonar and Radar programs, and at the Sensis Corporation on their Civilian Air Traffic programs.

Dan lives in Central New York and is the author of twelve books on Amazon KDP that address genealogy (1), the Korean War 1950 (1), engineering topics (9), and a Christmas play (1).

Songs

O Holy Night   86

O holy night, the stars are brightly shining,
It is the night of the dear Savior's birth;
Long lay the world in sin and error pining,
'Till he appeared, and the soul felt its worth.

A thrill of hope the weary world rejoices,
For yonder breaks a new and glorious morn;

Chorus
Fall on your knees, Oh hear the angel voices!
O night divine! O night when Christ was born.
O night, O holy night, O night divine.

Amazing Grace   24

Amazing Grace how sweet the sound
That saved a wretch like me
I once was lost, but now I'm found
Was blind but now I see

Twas grace that taught my heart to fear
And grace my fears relieved
How precious did that grace appear
The hour I first believed

36   Silent Night   72

Silent night, holy night
All is calm, all is bright
Round yon Virgin, Mother and Child
Holy infant so tender and mild
Sleep in heavenly peace
Sleep in heavenly peace

Silent night, holy night
Shepherds quake at the sight
Glories stream from Heaven afar
Heavenly hosts sing hallelujah
Christ the Savior is born
Christ the Savior is born

What Child is This   1

William Chatterton Dix wrote the lyrics to *What Child Is This* in 1865.

The song exists in many variants (lyrics and instruments).

This play utilizes the instrumental arrangement of artists John Morgan and Dave Fullen.
....
What child is this, who, laid to rest,
On Mary's lap is sleeping?
Whom angels greet with anthems sweet,
While shepherds watch are keeping.

This, this is Christ the King,
Whom shepherds guard and angels sing:
Haste, haste to bring him laud,
The babe, the son of Mary.

O Little Town of Bethlehem   56

O little town of Bethlehem,
How still we see thee lie.
Above thy deep and dreamless sleep
The silent stars go by;

Yet in thy dark streets shineth
The everlasting Light.
The hopes and fears of all the years
Are met in thee tonight.

Away in a Manger   59

Away in a manger,
No crib for His bed
The little Lord Jesus
Laid down His sweet head

The stars in the bright sky
Looked down where He lay
The little Lord Jesus
Asleep on the hay

Hallelujah   67
George Frideric Handel, Aneta Mihályová

Hallelujah! Hallelujah! Hallelujah!
Hallelujah! Hallelujah!

Hallelujah! Hallelujah! Hallelujah!
Hallelujah! Hallelujah!

For the Lord God Omnipotent reigneth

Hallelujah! Hallelujah! Hallelujah!
Hallelujah!

Hallelujah! Hallelujah! Hallelujah!
Hallelujah!

Hallelujah!

Matrimonial and Family Law

The Law Office
of
Denise Renee (Colasanti) Munson, Esq. PLLC

Denise Munson (March 23, 1966 – April 20, 2022)

Made in the USA
Middletown, DE
22 March 2024

51799134R00055